Hide and Seek

Tony Mitton

Illustrated by Andy Parker

one curly caterpillar

two big beetles

three green grasshoppers

four slippery snails

five little ladybirds

six wiggly worms

lots of laughing
little friends